T0128436

Little
Tragedies

Jennah Leach

Little Tragedies

Copyright © 2021 Jennah Leach.

All rights reserved. No part of this book may be used or reproduced by any means, graphic, electronic, or mechanical, including photocopying, recording, taping or by any information storage retrieval system without the written permission of the author except in the case of brief quotations embodied in critical articles and reviews.

iUniverse books may be ordered through booksellers or by contacting:

iUniverse
1663 Liberty Drive
Bloomington, IN 47403
www.iuniverse.com
844-349-9409

Because of the dynamic nature of the Internet, any web addresses or links contained in this book may have changed since publication and may no longer be valid. The views expressed in this work are solely those of the author and do not necessarily reflect the views of the publisher, and the publisher hereby disclaims any responsibility for them.

Any people depicted in stock imagery provided by Getty Images are models, and such images are being used for illustrative purposes only.
Certain stock imagery © Getty Images.

ISBN: 978-1-6632-2168-1 (sc)
ISBN: 978-1-6632-2169-8 (e)

Library of Congress Control Number: 2021915540

Print information available on the last page.

iUniverse rev. date: 08/11/2021

Seattle Weather

I waited until I couldn't remember what you looked like standing in front of me.
I thought it'd be easier than this.

Standing on the streets of Seattle, I wanted to tell you it was okay,
That it was human, falling out of love with me the way you did.
Your ring doesn't suit you anymore. I see it too.

This is not a poem.
This is me still crying at the syllables of your name,
And I can't breathe.
Can't breathe, can't breathe, can't breathe.

So I started and stopped
And stopped and stopped and stopped,
And then I rewrote it.

This is for you.

It was the way you didn't break me,
Not the way she broke you.
But it's been seven months,
And halfway through the third time seeing you, I'm reminded of standing on his front lawn again,
Feeling the buzz off of rash decisions and the sound of your voice inside the house.
I didn't see you that night.
Instead, I lit a cigarette with your name on it,
But you didn't burn out with it,
And the champagne only tastes like the gin you spiked it with.
I didn't know it then,
Watching you pack pot leaves into the spaces she left in you,
That you'd become the ache I couldn't suffocate or drown

—and it aches and aches.

Although you are the one who keeps coming back,
Maybe it is I who should let you go,
Stop whispering your name into the wind to make you turn my way,
Stop dreaming of sleeping next to you so you still wake up to the warmth.
I will let someone else's fingerprints replace mine across your skin.
And I will hope this pattern suits you better.
And I will hope the same for myself.

—and then I met him, and his car was white too.

I was in love with you.
That's why it made me sick to my stomach when you touched my skin,
And I prayed yours felt the same when you kissed me,
Prayed that you would never be high enough to say you didn't know
Because,
even drunk,
I knew you did not love me back.

The Boys with Blue Eyes

… and then you understood.
They're the color of his shirt the last time he kisses you,
The color of the state he left you in,
The ink that you wrote this with.

His eyes are the color of stars and oceans,
The lifetime that you saw pass between you.
It's all there in one glance
And then gone with the next.

Coffee Cups

To me it's just a cup of coffee,
But
I liked the way you smiled at the taste,
So I started sipping on it too,
And I thought how clever you must be after a few cups
Because my fascination with you was as simple as this.

K.S.

It was the way everything was gray before you,
Different shades of the same,
Muted, dulled.
But you moved like sunshine, bright and demanding,
And I had sworn, captivated in watching you, that this many colors never existed.

He spins words like magic,
And he thinks the world is his to use to his advantage
Because he's smug, but he's young, and he's charming and dangerous,
And his name is a legend passed between drinks and cigarettes,

And the girls chase after him like they stand a chance for more than one night,
But in the morning, he leaves them with a last kiss goodbye
Because he's beautiful, but he's tragic, and he's the wrong choice, you know,
But you smile around a cigarette and you let him pull you close,

But he drives too fast and he pretends the worst has already happened to him,
And you watch him get high enough to forget he's seen the bottom
Because he's smug, but he's young, and he's charming and dangerous,
And he laughs around his cigarette that life just is what it is,

So you kiss him like you stand a chance for more than tonight,
And when he leaves you, he doesn't tell you why
Because he's been broken in places that you aren't allowed to touch,
And he's distant, and he's brilliant, and he talks too much,

But he's learned to spin it all like magic,
And they think the world is his, but he doesn't have it
Because he's beautiful, but he's tragic, and life just is what it is,
But still, it makes you sad to look at him, doesn't it,
Because he looks away and it's easier to hide beneath the hype and the smoke,
And it takes the last cigarette in the pack for you to let him go.

We're like fireworks, him and I,
Colorful in sparks, and he's beautiful,
Intense for just a moment
Before we burn out gray
And there's too much smoke to keep track of each other for long.
But he has a voice that leaves my ears ringing all night.

I went back to him after you broke my heart.
God, it only took me a week.
I think I wanted him to hurt me.

I wanted him to pull me in
And kiss me like I still mattered to someone.
I wanted to get distracted by his laugh
And get drunk,
Share cigarettes at midnight,
Windows down and his song of the summer on repeat.

I know his lines.
I know he doesn't mean it.
But it keeps me sane for five more minutes.
I just wanted to feel something other than you.

SEATAC Airport

And when I got to the gate, I knew we'd never speak again.
I'd taken every flight of stairs like the distraction could keep me together.
It couldn't.
So I sat down
And I watched the sun come up over the mountains,
And then I cried in front of a thousand people that day,
But you weren't one of them.

I tell them that you were right; you were always right.
I tell them that I was so unhappy without you that I was too blinded to see it,
That I didn't realize you were unhappy too.
I tell them that long-distance relationships are hard,
That loving you from across the country is hard.
I tell them that I miss you,
That you weren't just my boyfriend
But that you were my future, all my plans and daydreams, and you were my friend.
I tell them I'm not mad at you,
And when they ask why,
I tell them that if you've done the right thing for you, how can I ask you for more than that?

—What you did was mean, but my opinion of you isn't.

I knew I was angry with you when I took the words I wrote for you
and gave them to another boy
Because his smile could light what you had dimmed inside my chest,
And like a match, together we sparked
Too fast and too slow,
Too blinded by the smoke to see the end held between his fingertips.
But my mind is a house of mirrors of you and him;
He's everywhere,
And your shadow clings to him.

It's not a feeling I recognize in myself,
Missing something.
But I'll keep the memory of you smiling as you kissed me goodbye and said you'd see me
later,
And I'll forget what happened after,
How you never did or what changed your mind
      Or how I've missed you since before you even pulled out of the parking lot.
I'm tired of being sad.
And I'm tired of crying when no one can see, and I'm tired of the way it aches to hear your
name.
So these will be the last words I'll write for you.
             I only wanted to see you happy,
               Artificial or not.

Most importantly, I now realize
It was the way you didn't take me seriously,
How you kept me within arm's reach and left me waiting there
But all you had to do was say sorry.
I think you knew,
And I'm too afraid to tell you I still miss you.

It will be the way I stop saying your name
Out of longing or out of boredom,
And in those moments, I'll remember.
Maybe I was a little bit in love with you
Or maybe I was in love with the ways you were different than me,
The way you mesmerized anyone you spoke to.
You are still one of the loveliest things I've ever seen.

These are the ways I'll let you become a part of me,
And I think you knew this would happen.
I think you knew.

I never knew how to make it sound pretty,
Too much cigarette ash and smudged pen ink,
But it's 1:00 a.m.
And I want you to let me prick myself along the sharp edges of you
And trace maps into my skin.
Tell me this is the safest place for us
Even though you're a mess just like me,
And I'll describe it all just like a kiss …

But it's 1:00 a.m.,
And your words are prettier than mine.

—I've been drunk for weeks.

You said that when you left,
it was like you'd taken the Florida weather with you,

And maybe that was true
Because six months later, you still looked like sunshine.
I always described you in shades of yellow.

But I had sworn, the week you left me,
It was like I'd taken the Seattle weather with me,

And I slept in dark gray sheets,
Pulling colors from the threads of strangers,
But none of them were right.

It feels like a lightning bolt through my chest.

You were—
We.
We were such a struggle.

But the ache doesn't reach down to my bones now,

And it happens all at once,
Where I stop trying to replace you with strangers
Because I was lonely.
I wasn't heartbroken anymore.

She's like a bruise, you said,
Black and blue and tinged with red,
And she caught you off guard,
So you took the hit harder than you expected, didn't you?
Felt her burrow under your skin unlike anything else before,
Just fingerprints at first,
But you'd rather rip yourself open,
Either to try and bleed her out
Or to keep her alive,
Watching her stain everything you touch,
Painting other women in the shape of her.
You're letting her spread;
Her handprints are all over you now.

I imagine us meeting again
Years from now when I don't consider us kids anymore,
When we're not hung up on should-bes or caught in the ideas of each other,
Dreaming out loud of a perfect life together.
If only we could touch the same place at the same time
And we don't meet as lovers of the past
But as friends, I think, who have parted ways for now.
It tastes bittersweet to say I imagine you happy with someone else.

I searched for the words to describe you in poetry books,
First in one,
Then in eight more,
And then eleven more,
And when I couldn't find you in their pages,
And lost you for the second time,
I wrote you one instead.

Apollo

In the middle of the afternoon,
Listening to the same playlist
And lying next to your best friend,

This is the moment

He puts his arm around your shoulders,
Laughs when he kisses your cheek,
And suddenly he's everything to you.

I'm not heartbroken by your absence.
I'm too exhausted to be.
It's disappointment, I guess,
At the promises I didn't ask for but believed because they came from you,
At the spaces I made for you just for you to leave them empty,
At the way you used the word *love* without being ready for it,
And it eats away at my stomach until I'm too sick to feel anything else.

G.K.

Look me in the eyes.
I want to see galaxies
And explosions.
I want to see the world end with you next to me,
And we'll be in awe over the colors we create in the darkness,
The way you trace new constellations into my skin every life we meet,
All the miles you've traveled for me,
And I'll trail stardust down your body with my lips
Until you shimmer the prettiest shades of the universe.

And palm to palm,
Our fingers laced together,
This is how it feels when stars collide.

How can your hands be so soft with me
But so cruel with the world?
You dig them graves and leave bloodstains
With the same fingers that touch me like a rose petal,
Thinking I might mistake the dirt smudges from the flowers you plant at my feet.

And your voice is faded, but I hear "I love you,"
The last taunt that echoes in the empty room.
What I meant to say is I love you too,
But you already knew.

He asks you what you think the meaning of life is.
You're both only twenty-two.
It's almost midnight, and as a ritual you smoke a cigarette together after work.
And the answer is easy back then.
It's to find your soulmate.
But he tells you that you're not thinking hard enough.

You're twenty-three when he asks you if you think you know what love is.
You've gotten into the habit of mixing alcohol with your tobacco.
Betrayed, like every young adult, by the fairytales that raised you,
You say no,
But that's what it should be like.
He tells you that you're still learning to love yourself.

You're twenty-four the first real time your heart gets broken,
And it feels so shattered that the pieces catch in your throat every time you breathe,
So you don't say his name for a year,
And he shakes his head at you
But orders another round,
Fills the astray at the bar with you,
And lets you forget that his heart is broken too,
All for a boy who never stopped to think of how cold he'd left you,
And he asks you if this is still what love looks like to you.

He asks you what the meaning of life is,
Already three lives in by the time he's twenty-six,
And now you say you don't know.
There are scabs over old wounds and soulmates are friends.
No drinks anymore, and now he vapes.
There's a calm feeling you bring out in each other,
And you tell him that maybe life is just life.
You've grown tired of thinking.

Come home to me.
Let me be careful with you.
Your thoughts are too rough on your body.

I'd describe it like seeing the light at the end of the tunnel
After you've been spinning in the dark for years,
Tapping at the walls for secret passageways that never existed
And crawling over rocks and the bones of the people you've outgrown.
And then suddenly
You just see it.

That's how I feel about you.

You always said we were a matter of when,
Never if.
So tomorrow
Or next year,
Ten years from now,
You were going to have me.
After all this time
I guess you were right.

All my first kisses have been in the middle of the night.
I thought it was mysterious and romantic

Until he kissed me at four thirty in the morning
And I didn't realize he was made of the shadows,
All smudged lines and secret thoughts.

But then you kissed me in the afternoon,
The sun in your hair like a halo,
And I never saw the darkness coming.

I started craving you in a crowded room,
And now I can't breathe without you in my lungs,
Can't focus thinking about you out of my reach
Or calm the panic that settles in my hands,
And they say you're bad for me,
Killing me in places I haven't thought of.
The burns are small prices to pay to be close to you.
I can't quit.

Light me up.

You look like mine,
Covered in dark blue and my teeth marks all over your skin.
Even strangers can see the way I stain your lips.

You feel like mine,
And you feel like home
With your leg between my thighs and my fingers through your hair.

It's taken us five years,
But I should've warned you
That if you kiss me, I'll fall in love with you,
That you'll look like mine.

You touched me with dark pinks
And layers of purples and golds,
Finger painting streaks of vivid colors onto a blank canvas,
Begging me to see a masterpiece,
But all I see is the paint dripping,
And now your hands are the same muddied color as my mind.

You left the blankets in the same tangled mess you left me,
And I slept like that for weeks,
Trying to pull everything back into its place,
Trying to guess if you missed me too.

I miss you.
I'm drunk and I'm lonely for you
And I'm thinking about your laugh.
How stupid.
How simple.
But I'm sitting on the floor
With a glass of rosé wine and a cigarette,
And I feel warm
And I feel like I'm alive.

I've never heard you this quiet.
I don't know what to do.
Nothing works.
You're so sad.
And I'm sad too.

You soak me to the bone.
I never thought that my temper could singe your fingertips when you reached for me,
Was never worried of the marks you could leave behind if you wanted to

Because we met at the edge,
Daring life so dangerously that we laughed at the idea of ever being ghosts to each other,
And I was never afraid of loving you too much
Until I fell in love with you.

But your soul bleeds into mine,
And after the first touch, it all made sense,
Why I'd keep you at such a distance from me.

We burn too bright together,
Flashing through the centuries we've circled each other,
Feeling everything all at once until it consumes the last of us,
Until we both go dark.

I thought about calling you before the ink even had a chance to dry,
But an hour goes by
And I still can't keep calm enough for a moment,
Pacing the room and staring at your name
Because I've been spiraling down too
And I've been making new life plans too,
But I know you'll never listen when you're like this.

So I wrote you poems about stars and promises
Of me being here always,
And I hoped that these would be enough.

I fell in love with you.
I don't know how it happened either.
Just say you love me too.
Tell me forever.

I cried once in the shower
After a particularly hard day,
And I cried myself to sleep the first night,
Thinking about you,
But of all the cliché things
I should've cried on the phone with you
So you could hear what I couldn't say with words.
Maybe then you'd understand.

You made a home in my ribcage,
Rattling your bones against mine until they ache,
Invading my thoughts,
And crawling through my veins,
Pulsing your heartbeat into mine.
You're making noise for my attention,
Screaming until it echoes from the bottom of my bottle
And crying hard enough to make my hands shake.
But my lungs can't breathe you out.
You twist your fingers between my ribs,
And you gather me in close
Just to tell me that I'm the one keeping you prisoner.

I envision the hands I have all over you,
Metaphorically,
And one by one,
Week by week,
My fingers loosen their grip.

I'm running out of ways to say I love you.

Stay with me.
I'm your best friend.

Where else would we go
if it wasn't together?

That's all I wanted to say.
I just wish I knew how to make it sound like poetry.

One more drink
And maybe I'll get the words out.

This is different
With us
This time, I'm sure.

You're supposed to be with me
And you know it.

You're made of little tragedies,
Violent swirls of chaos and gray
In a costume of human skin,
Handing pieces of your rain cloud to people like a gift,
Giving back to the world what it's given to you.

So I've done the only thing I can think of
With a love as messy as yours.
I tore my heart out,
Tear stained and bloody,
And I offered you the last tragedy I had left,
Hoping you'd accept the gift.

Sleep with me.
I'm too tired to wake up alone again.

We aren't soulmates,
But I desperately wish we were.
Maybe it'd explain why we're so crazy with each other.

You ask her to love you,
And it's selfish the way you leave your tears in her lap,
But your sadness is too much to hold on your own.

And then you ask her to wait
Because your body is here,
Alive and soft, breathing easy in her arms,
But your mind is still in the past,
Your vision blurred around her edges.

And when you feel like you have nothing left to give her,
Shrinking so far into yourself that she almost mistakes it for being on your knees,
You ask her to still be your friend.

I don't know if I'd call it brave
Or if I'd just say it's hopeless,
The way you stood next to me all these years
With a backbone strong enough to carry us both.
You loved me blindly
When I couldn't see a reason to,
And maybe now it's my turn to do the same.

Tonight, I'm mad at you,
Bent so far out of shape
That I don't even recognize myself.

Tonight, I'm in love with you,
My thoughts twisted and strained
Into broken heart shapes of you.

Tonight, I see shapes that don't exist,
Trying to make sense of what's left of us now.

I poured my life into words,
The black ink like a pair of lungs,
Because this is how I learned to breathe.

But then my heart spilled onto the page,
And before I could clean up the mess,
You saw it.

You're a daydream,
Filling my head with pretty ideas.
I can't think of anything else.

It's normal until it isn't.
We try to act like it's the same,
But it's not.
We aren't just friends anymore,
And your body comes back to mine
With a sigh of relief.

And I don't know which is worse:
Having half of you
Or not having you at all.

The clouds come in with you,
And there's lightning every time my eyes meet yours.
Trying to keep the bolts from hitting too close to home,
My heartbeat sounds like thunder to my ears,
And there's static where we used to talk.
But my hands brush the raindrops from your hair,
Waiting for the storm to pass.

I love you.
This is what you wanted.
I don't understand.

—When he leaves you.

What the hell.

Dolphin

All the parts of her that sparkle are dull inside me.
She wouldn't lay a hand on anyone, but I'm still trying to clean the blood from underneath my fingernails.
And even though her body is sick, my soul is the thing that's already rotting.
How could this happen to you,
Where you're in love with two dead girls
At once?

We don't exist in the same room together.
We're just shadows of each other,
And we're being eclipsed
By you,
Always looking over your shoulder,
Always looking for a way to bottle the light behind you.
But you'll get dizzy going around and around like this,
Trying to hold both of us.

I promised you I'd always be your best friend,
But I never told you how much it'd hurt me
Or all my failed attempts to keep you from caving in
And the dirt on my clothes,
Trying to talk you out of the grave you'd dug
For you and her.

She's his lifeline,
And he's wrapped himself in tightly,
Twisting her around his thoughts like a crown
And tethering himself to her fate.

Don't you see
That as she dies,
He slowly dies with her?

Let me go first
And keep her
Because now I can't get her out of my mind either.
She's written all over you,
Anywhere I touch,
And I can't see a way for me to fit.

Call her
And tell her you love her.
Tell her how you wish things were different.
I'll still be here when you hang up.

I would change your reality.
I would rewind time and take her place
Without so much as a backwards glance.
And I've never lied to you,
But how could I tell you the truth,
That I would trade my life for hers
For you.

The only thing that's going to make it better is time.
Two years have passed,
And I caught myself laughing for the first time telling a story about him.
What I'm trying to say
Is that one day you'll talk about her,
And it won't always be easy,
But it won't be like reliving it over and over.

And the real tragedy of us
Is that we were in love at the same time,
But you told me you loved her first
And you chose her.

Your body will get numb to the feeling,
So tired of suffering
That you'll forget it's supposed to hurt,
Until you're happy without them.

And then it hits you twice as hard,
When you can't decide if the person next to you
Is the wrong one.

I know you're not ready,
That you think letting her go means she's meant less to you,
But it doesn't.
And I know you don't want to hear this
Because you feel guilty for it,
But you are moving on
And you are changing.
That's why it hurts so much.

Love her while you can.
I'll understand.

I saw the *M* in your pills years ago.
You grabbed my arm and stamped the *A* onto my skin.
When you asked me not to leave you alone on your birthday,
I found a *D* in the way you compared her love to anyone else's,
And the other *D* lit up in front of my face like a warning sign.
I'm always left feeling like your second thought,
So when the *Y* fell out of your shirt and landed between us,
I told you that it was okay;
Your heart is still shedding pieces of her.

Love Letter to His First Love

He's still the same sweet boy. And he says your name with a softness that will last forever. I hope you read this and know that he's loved. I'll take care of him. I promise you.

Printed in the United States
by Baker & Taylor Publisher Services